The
FIVE SENSES

Troll Associates

The
FIVE SENSES

by Keith Brandt

Illustrated by Gloria Green

Troll Associates

Library of Congress Cataloging in Publication Data

Brandt, Keith, (date)
Five senses.

Summary: Describes how the information collectors
known as our sense organs send messages to the brain
which are interpreted for us as seeing, hearing, tasting,
smelling, and feeling.
1. Senses and sensation—Juvenile literature.
[1. Senses and sensation] I. Green, Gloria, ill.
II. Title.
QP434.B73   1984   612'.8   84-2633
ISBN 0-8167-0168-7 (lib. bdg.)
ISBN 0-8167-0169-5 (pbk.)

It's a bright, sunshiny day. You sit on the
cool grass, eating a pretzel and listening to
the buzzing of a bee. You reach out to pick a
sweet-smelling red rose, and as you grasp the
stem—ouch! A thorn sticks your finger. You
quickly pull your hand back. So much is
going on, and you are aware of it all. You can
see, hear, smell, taste, and touch because you
are using your five senses.

You can see the sun shining because of your sense of *sight*. You are using special sense organs called your eyes. You can hear the sound of the bee buzzing because of your sense of *hearing*. You are using sense organs called your ears.

You are aware of the sweet aroma of the rose because of your sense of *smell*. It is in the sense organ called your nose. You can feel the sharpness of the thorn because of your sense of *touch*, which is in the organ called your skin. And you can tell that the pretzel is salty because of your sense of *taste*. You taste things through sense organs called taste buds, which are located in your tongue.

Your sense organs are connected to your brain by a system of nerves. Each sense organ sends messages through your nerves, telling your brain what is happening. But it is your brain that sees, hears, tastes, feels, and smells.

For example, when your hand comes near a hot stove, the nerve endings on your skin sense the heat. A message is sent through your nerves to your brain. Instantly, your brain receives the information and decodes it. Only then do you feel the heat. Your brain flashes back a message, and you quickly pull your hand away.

Your sense organs are really information collectors. Your brain must interpret that information. So you do not actually see, hear, taste, smell, or feel until your brain gets the message.

Your brain is like the most complicated computer. It never stops receiving, decoding, and sending out messages. Even when you're asleep, your brain is hearing, smelling, feeling, and so on. It is constantly alert to all signals. But it won't wake you unless one of the senses tells it there is a reason to get up.

Suppose a telephone rings and you hear the sound. What actually happens as you use your sense of hearing? The sound waves made by the telephone are collected by your *outer ear* and directed toward your *eardrum*. Your eardrum is a thin sheet of tissue stretched across a passage in your ear. The sound waves make your eardrum vibrate, like the skin on a drum when you hit it.

The sound is then carried into the *middle ear*, where there are three loosely attached small bones. They vibrate too.

Now the sound passes on to the *inner ear*. Inside the inner ear is the *cochlea*, a tube shaped like a snail's shell, which is filled with a watery liquid. The liquid in the cochlea vibrates, and this, in turn, vibrates thousands of tiny hair cells, which are also in the cochlea.

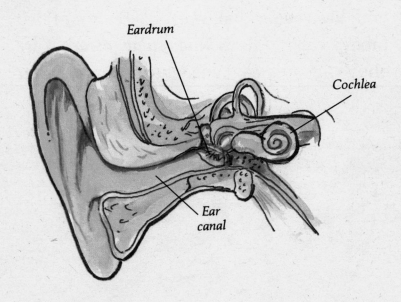

Eardrum

Cochlea

Ear canal

The hair cells are connected to the brain by nerves called *auditory nerves*. These auditory nerves carry the message in the form of electrical impulses to the brain.

The brain receives and decodes these impulses and turns them into sounds. And the whole process—from the telephone's ring to your brain hearing it—happens in an instant.

Besides being the sense organ of hearing, each ear contains three small tubes that help you keep your balance. These fluid-filled tubes, called the *semicircular canals*, are above the cochlea. Whenever you move your

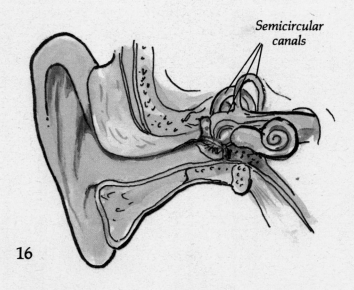

Semicircular canals

head, the fluid moves too. And the movement changes the pressure in the semi-circular canals. This message is sent through the nerves to the brain, which sends back information that helps you keep your balance.

What happens when you use your sense of sight? Suppose, for example, your eyes are looking at a tree. There are rays of light hitting the tree. Without light you cannot see anything. The light rays make up the image of the tree. These light rays enter your eyes through a clear covering called the *cornea.*

Then the rays pass through an opening in your eye called the *pupil*. Surrounding the pupil is the colored part of the eye called the *iris*. The iris has muscles that make the pupil larger in dim light and smaller in bright light, so that just the right amount of light is let in.

Behind the pupil is the *lens*. The lens focuses the image of the tree on a tissue called the *retina*. The retina is located at the back of the eyeball. The retina is connected to *optic nerves* that lead to the brain. The tree you are looking at is right-side up. But the lens focuses its image on the retina upside down. Your brain, however, corrects the picture so that you see the tree the way it really is.

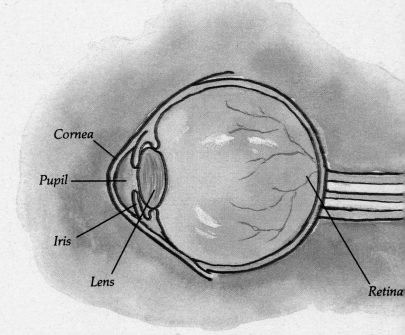

Cornea

Pupil

Iris

Lens

Retina

What happens when you use your sense of taste? How do you know that a piece of chocolate is sweet, not salty like a pretzel or sour like a lemon? Your taste buds collect information about the chocolate and send that information to your brain.

There are four kinds of taste buds, and they are all on your tongue. The taste buds on the tip of your tongue are most sensitive to sweetness. But the tip of your tongue can also taste salt. So can the sides of your tongue, which are also sensitive to sour tastes. The back of your tongue is most sensitive to bitter tastes. The center of the tongue has no taste buds at all.

The tongue also passes on information about temperature and texture of the food you are eating. These facts and the tastes are all instantly sent to the brain. The brain then decodes the message and tells you what you are tasting.

Sometimes, when you have a cold and a stuffy nose, food seems tasteless. That is because much of the taste of food depends on its smell. In fact, if you close your eyes and hold your nose tightly, you may not be able to tell the difference between the taste of an onion and the taste of an apple.

Your sense of smell works through the sense organ called your nose. Smells reach your nose because there are tiny gas particles in the air. When you breathe in, these particles enter your nasal, or nose, passages and reach your smell cells. Your smell cells are called the *olfactory cells*.

The olfactory cells send messages through nerve cells to the brain. Then the brain identifies the odor and tells you what you are smelling. When you eat, gas particles released by the food send these messages to your brain. So as you eat your food, you taste it *and* smell it.

Probably the most complex sense of all is the sense of touch, which uses the largest organ you have: your skin. Through your skin you can feel if an object is hard or soft, rough or smooth, wet or dry, hot or cold, tight or loose, sharp or blunt. You can tell if what you are touching is made of wood, plastic, metal, cloth, liquid, and so on.

Sensory receptors, or nerve endings in your skin, receive messages and send them through your nervous system to your brain. Your brain then identifies what your skin is touching.

There are different receptors for different feelings. Some are sensitive to pain; others are sensitive to heat and cold; and still others are sensitive to pressure.

There are more pain receptors than any other kind, because pain tells the brain that something bad has happened to the body. It may be as minor as a scratch from a thorn, or as serious as a broken leg. But the body must have this information right away or it won't be able to react and try to help itself.

Messages of pain are also sent to the brain from nerve endings inside the body. They report on stomachaches, headaches, muscle soreness, bone breaks, toothaches, and other big and little problems.

If you eat too much and your stomach hurts, the pain you feel is real. At the same time, you know that the cause is not something serious, and that the pain will soon disappear. But if you have a toothache, it is a clear signal that you must go to the dentist. Nerve endings inside the body also send messages that tell you when you are hungry or thirsty or tired.

Every day a million things happen all around you. But they don't mean anything to you until you are aware of them. That marvelous computer called your brain tells you all about odors, textures, and tastes. It tells you what you are looking at and listening to. But it couldn't do a thing without your sense organs—those wonderful organs of sight, sound, smell, taste, and touch.